Sculpture Kahlil Gibran

SCULPTURE

KAHLIL GIBRAN

With a Foreword by

Dr. Evan H. Turner

Director

Philadelphia Museum of Art

The Bartlett Press • Publishers • Boston

First Edition

Library of Congress Catalogue Card Number 71-130940
Manufactured in the United States of America

Acknowledgments

My thanks for their encouragement and counsel in the creation of this book go to Mr. Abraham Bornstein of the Boston Book & Art Shop; Mr. Morton C. Bradley, Jr., collector and mentor; Mr. Stuart Denenberg, art dealer; Mr. James Mead, collector; Dr. Evan H. Turner, Director of the Philadelphia Museum of Art; and to my wife, Jean.

Foreword

The young artist such as Kahlil Gibran coming of age intellectually and aesthetically in the years following the second World War was faced with a perplexing dilemma. The artist's responsibility to confront specific subjects was being questioned with the energetic doubts that challenged so many other traditional ideals. Given his own background of a dedicated spiritual involvement and his fascination with not only the distinguished achievements of the history of art but also the curious exceptions in that evolution, Kahlil Gibran chose to pursue a dialogue with subject; thus it was that he attacked the challenge of his own creative development with the nervous energy, with the taste, and with the technical skill that has characterized his work ever since.

A series of exquisitely painted canvases in the late 1940s which presented various natural phenomena in a grandly lyrical context could leave no doubt at that time of his able imagination. But clearly, as time has shown, the excitement of discovering forms, then emerging from the elegant diaphanous painted surfaces, was to become his primary concern. With great care during the two decades since then, this artist has developed a succession of highly expressive sculptures which have reflected a great commitment to the aesthetic standards of the past while expressing his own deeply felt concern for humanity or, more privately, his delight in life's joys. And while these sculptures are by no means all that he has created during these years, they have been, to him, his most important achievement.

The specific demands of sculpture are such that the responsible artist has no choice but to solve its technical problems if he is to achieve success. Kahlil Gibran has certainly invested incredible care in the realization of his figures. In fact the most significant factor of evolution apparent in his work as a whole is the steadily increasing technical facility.

Early in the 1950s he began with fascinating original results to explore the idea of suggesting three-dimensional form through creating a linear network built up with an incredible delicacy. The resulting ingenious complexity of texture giving at any distance a constantly shifting effect to the surfaces of the entire work may have been suggested by his interest in drawing techniques — because in many of the pieces the form does in fact seem built up in a manner not dissimilar to that of such great draftsmen as Albrecht Dürer or his Flemish predecessors.

Simultaneously he began exploring the description of form through the most subtle modeling of metal planes. The undulating surfaces of such a superb work as the small *Young Trunk* present an extraordinarily happy combination of achievement in this technique complementing a beauty of outlook. In the most ambitious of the larger works his reticulated surfaces are joined with metal sheets to create dramatic results. The large *Figure,* for example, achieves an expressiveness dependent upon the ingenious sophistication of his technical skills. The attention to every nuance imposed earlier upon the young artist as he created superb musical instruments has stood the mature artist in good stead.

Such absolute flexibility gives Kahlil Gibran a marvelous freedom to pursue the ideas dominating his works. The results leave today's overly assaulted public no choice but to become involved. His work is dedicated to quest — but his is a quest, expressed though it may be in terms of highly traditional subjects, that is thoroughly contemporary in its sense of concern.

It is hardly by chance that so many of his most important works deal with those Biblical figures — John the Baptist, Job, and David — whose search for truth was the dominant direction of their lives. His most ambitious piece, the ingeniously designed *Pieta,* presents the grief-stricken confusion of the living Mother as she contemplates the sad result of her Son's sacrifice demanded by His search for truth through salvation.

The power of these monumental figures is nurtured by the wonderful humanity of the artist and it is this quality which is repeatedly the keynote in the smaller works. The variety of expressiveness in the totality of his works inevitably nurtures the respect the artist richly deserves and, much more to the point, assures a profound involvement in Gibran's own conflict — his anguish of concern and his delight in experience.

Evan H. Turner
Director
Philadelphia Museum of Art

Contents

Self Portrait • Bronze • 5 Inch Diameter

SCULPTURE

KAHLIL GIBRAN

Biography

1922	Born in Boston, Son of Rose and Nicholas Gibran.
1930-1940	Worked with his father, a cabinet maker and craftsman.
1940-1943	Entered Boston Museum School of Fine Arts. Studied with Karl Zerbe. Awarded school scholarships and prizes.
1944, 1945	Worked as a draftsman at Underwater Sound Laboratory, Harvard University.
1945	Established studio in Boston. Supported career by making instruments, carving and gilding for local museums. Exhibited paintings at Stuart Art Gallery, Boston.
1946	Exhibited at Niveau Gallery, New York.
1947	Exhibited at Worcester Art Museum and at Jacques Seligmann Gallery, New York.

1948	**One man show at Charles Smith Gallery, Boston. Exhibited at Whitney Annual, New York.**
1949-1953	**Spent summers painting in Provincetown, Mass.**
1949	**One Man Show of paintings at Mortimer Levitt Gallery, New York, Exhibited at Carnegie Institute, Pittsburgh; Institute of Contemporary Art, Boston; Gulf Coast Circuit Show, Florida.**
1950	**Exhibited at Mortimer Levitt Gallery, New York.**
1951, 1952	**One man show at Margaret Brown Gallery, Boston.**
1953	**Summered and exhibited in Nantucket.**
1954	**Exhibited at Museum of Art, Rhode Island School of Design.**
1955	**Began welded sculpture.**
1956	**Popular Prize for *John the Baptist* at Boston Arts Festival.**
1958	**George D. Widener Gold Medal, Pennsylvania Academy, for *Voice in the Wilderness*. Exhibited at Art U.S.A., New York; Washington Cathedral, Washington, D.C.; Contem-**

porary Arts Museum, Houston, Texas; Dallas Museum of Fine Arts.

1959 Awarded John Simon Guggenheim Fellowship. Exhibited at Munson-Williams-Proctor Institute, Utica, New York; Jacques Seligmann Gallery, New York; University of Illinois.

1960 Renewal of Guggenheim Grant. Exhibited sculpture in Whitney Annual, New York.

1961 National Institute of Arts and Letters Award. Exhibited at Art Institute of Chicago.

1962 One man sculpture show at Lee Nordness Gallery, New York.

1964 Grand Prize, Boston Arts Festival for *Young Trunk*. Exhibited at Cheekwood Museum, Tennessee Fine Arts Center, Nashville.

1965 John Gregory Award for Sculpture awarded at National Sculpture Society. Exhibited at Montreal Museum of Fine Arts.

1966 Awarded Gold Medal for Excellence at 2nd International Show of Religious Art, Trieste, Italy.

1967	*Standing Figure* exhibited at Obelisk Gallery, Boston.
1968	*Reclining Nude* exhibited at New England Sculpture Society, Prudential Center, Boston.
1969	One man show of bronze plaques and drawings at Cambridge Art Association.

Direction and Purpose

John the Baptist, my first welded figure, grew out of a fascination for a jumble of baling wire discovered on a Boston wharf. His staff — a tie rod for piers — was eroded by the sea into a most beautifully organic and tactile iron length. The figure was already there. All that was required was order. It was all there, the conceptual and the technical — the raw and primal qualities of John in the desert reflected through nature's brutalization of man's objects. John rose from the heat of the torch, and in me rose a dedication to the intensity of this technique as a means of expressing my deepest feelings concerning man. The acetylene torch is an innovative tool of the twentieth century, a catalyst for the sculptor and his ideas. This alchemical device, evoking the medieval search for truth, held a primordial and mystical appeal for me. The immediacy of fire on iron created in my work an initial brutality of form, which I later refined through the gradual inclusion of the smooth iron sheet to a happy balance of rod and sheet in *Pieta*.

This afforded me a language I could most easily live with and use. This tactile and visual contrast gives further tonality to my expression and opportunity for another dimension to my language in sculpture. Its immediacy relieved me of the tedium of the long plaster-bronze visualization process with its attendant surface handling by others — chasers, patiners, etc. The welding surfaces are my expressions alone, and I trust that this medium is truly an intrinsic tool of my message.

My subject matter is man first and foremost, and I am weighted heavily by the sobriety of life as I have seen it and felt it. My interpretations of emotions are resolved as basically as I am able. I try to ignore the literal depiction of feelings but do use the human form as the vehicle in my search for a universal statement. I have selected historical figures as subjects knowing that man's essential concerns are timeless.

After the completion of *Reclining Nude*, the last welded piece in this book, I devoted myself for two years to a series of mixed media drawings as a much needed respite from the extreme physical abuse that welded and hammered sculpture exacted of me. My return to sculpture was to be a slow withdrawal from the linear and two-dimensional world of drawing, through the medium of bas relief modeled in wax and cast in bronze. Bas relief — a form beautifully positioned between drawing and sculpture in the round. I enjoyed the intimacy of the small format and the tenderness, subtlety and restraint required by the infinite variety of the shallow surface. My creative life became infinitely richer when it encompassed conceptual polarities: the shallow forms contrasting with the full round, the restraint of energy in drawing with the exhausting physical effort in hammering steel. Thus I humbly present the plates in this book.

Kahlil Gibran

SCULPTURE

John the Baptist

Welded Iron Rod
Height 7 Feet

1956

NORFOLK VA.
Collection Chrysler Museum, ~~Provincetown, Massachusetts~~

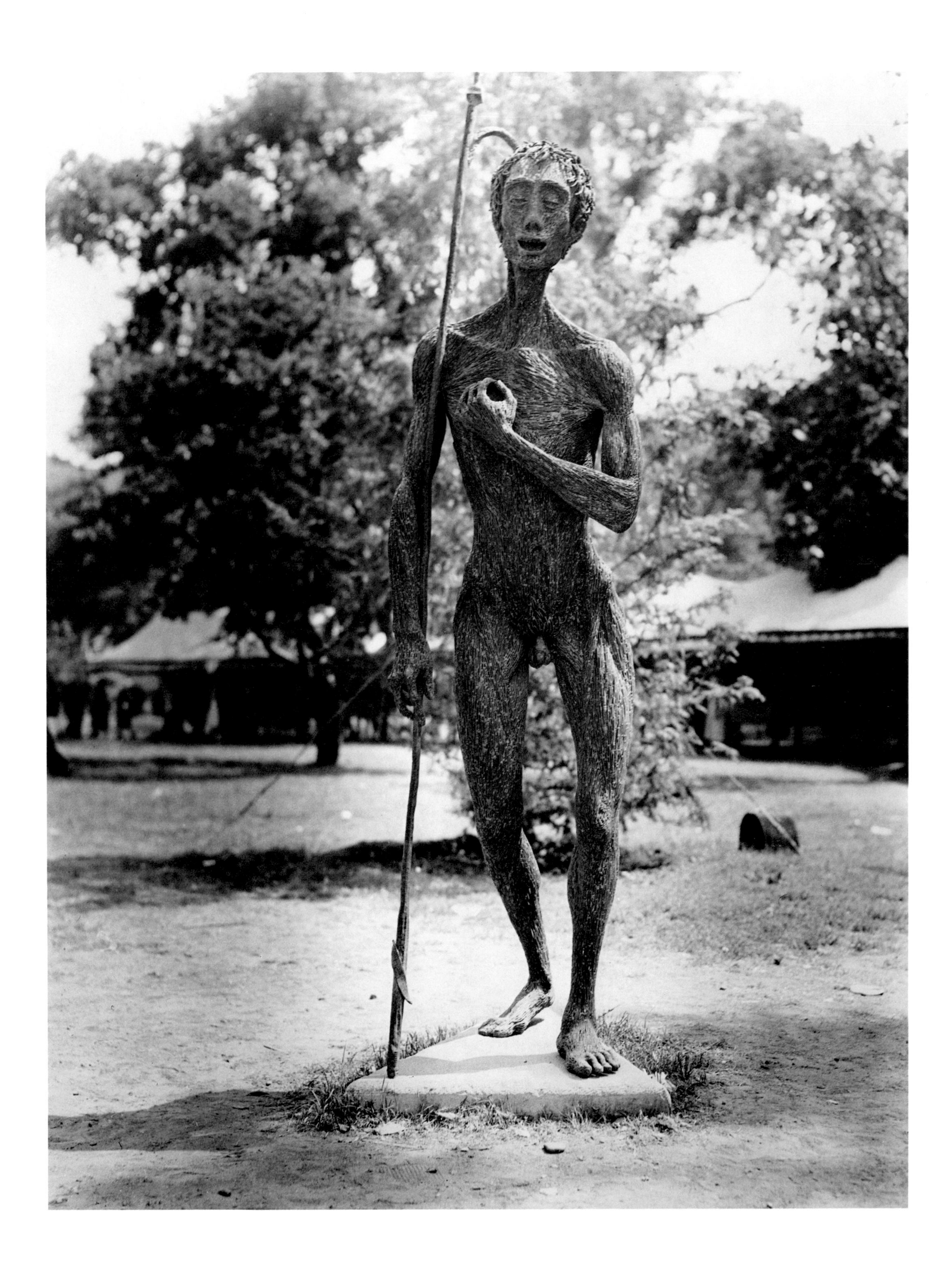

John the Baptist

Detail

John the Baptist

Detail

John the Baptist

Detail

Ferocious Mask

Welded Steel
Height 10 Inches

1956

Collection Museum of Fine Arts, Norfolk, Virginia

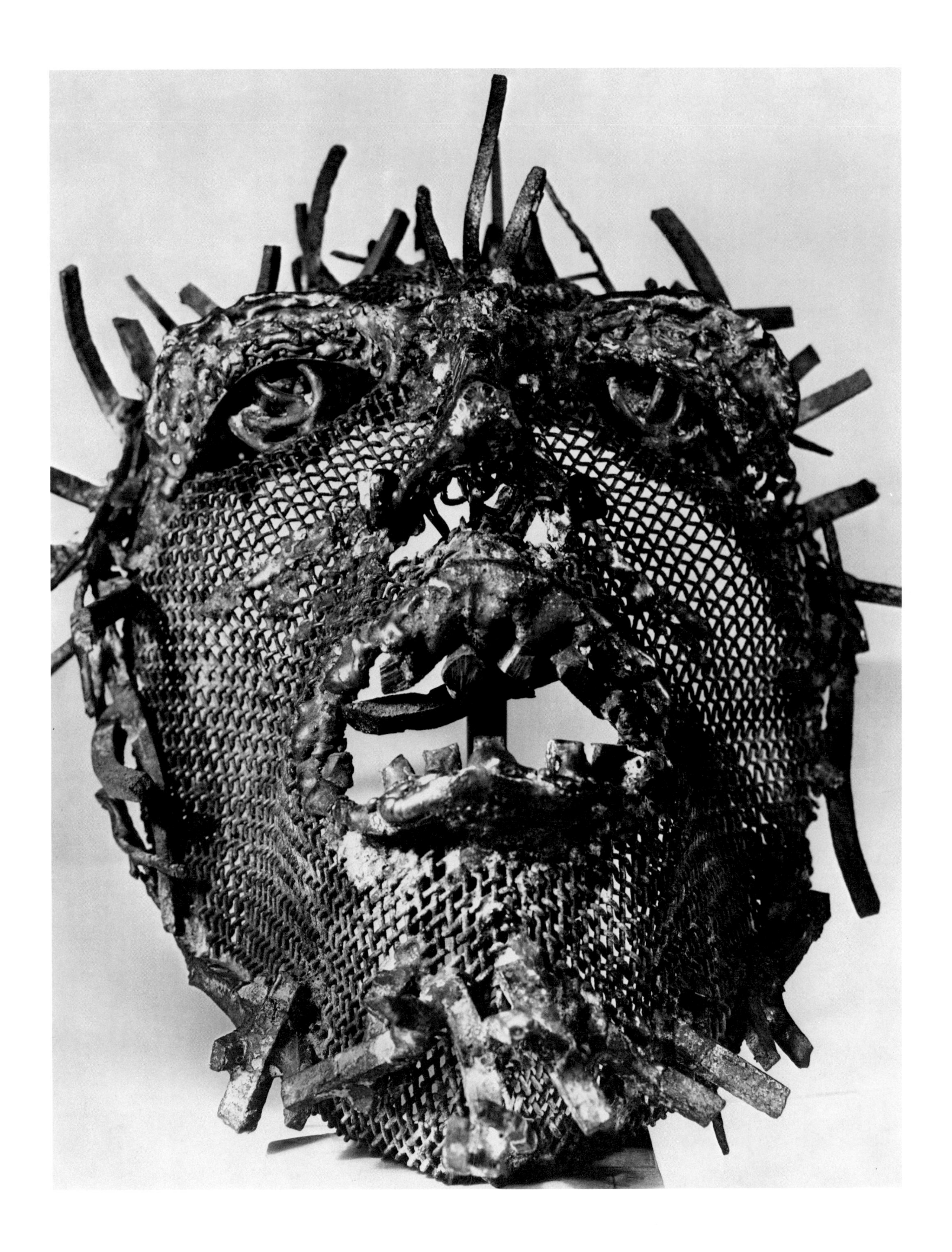

Bronze Study

Welded Bronze
Height 4 Inches

1957

Collection Dr. and Mrs. Malcolm Bick, Springfield, Massachusetts

Portrait in Wire

Welded Iron Rod
Height 16 Inches

1957

MARSTON MILLS CAPE COD
Collection Mrs. Herbert C. Morris, ~~Philadelphia, Pennsylvania~~

Voice in the Wilderness

Welded Iron Rod
Height 7 Feet

1957

Collection Pennsylvania Academy of Fine Arts, Philadelphia, Pennsylvania

Man Walking

Brazed Iron Wire
Height 15 Inches

1958

FLA.

Collection Mr. and Mrs. Bernard Singer, ~~Newton~~, ~~Massachusetts~~

Man Walking

Detail

Job

Welded Iron Rod
Height 16 Inches

1958

Collection Mrs. Jerry Goldberg, ~~Brookline~~, ~~Massachusetts~~

Job

Side View

Study of a Friend

Welded Bronze
Height 10 Inches

1958

Collection Dr. and Mrs. Victor Auerbach, Ambler, Pennsylvania

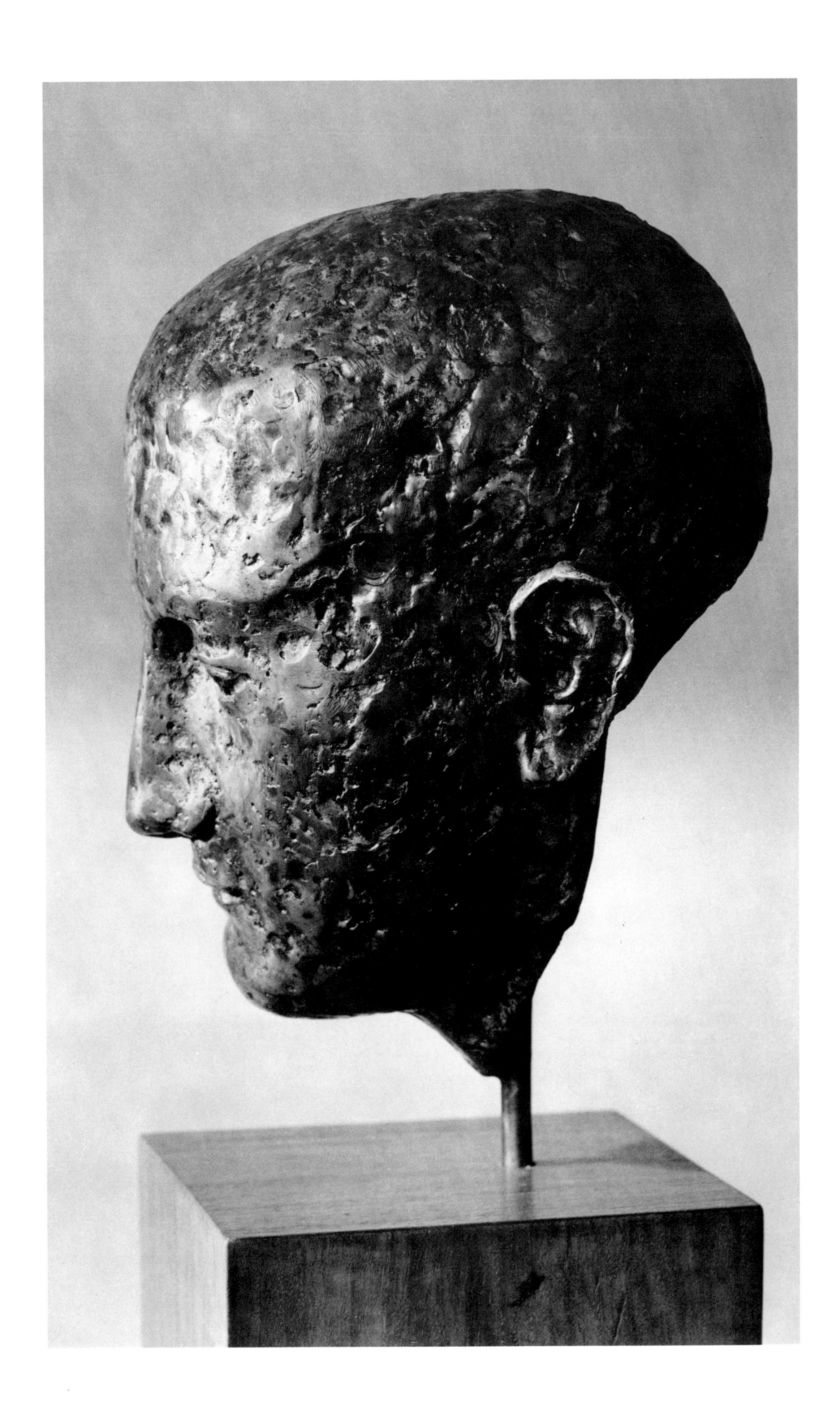

Wall Figure

Welded Bronze
Height 24 Inches

1958

of Dr. Bick Springfield MASS.

Collection ~~Mr. and Mrs. Leon Cohen~~, ~~Lakeland~~, ~~Florida~~

Fragmented Figure

Hammered Steel
Height 12 Inches

1958

Collection Dr. and Mrs. Walter Abelmann, ~~Lexington~~ BOSTON, Massachusetts

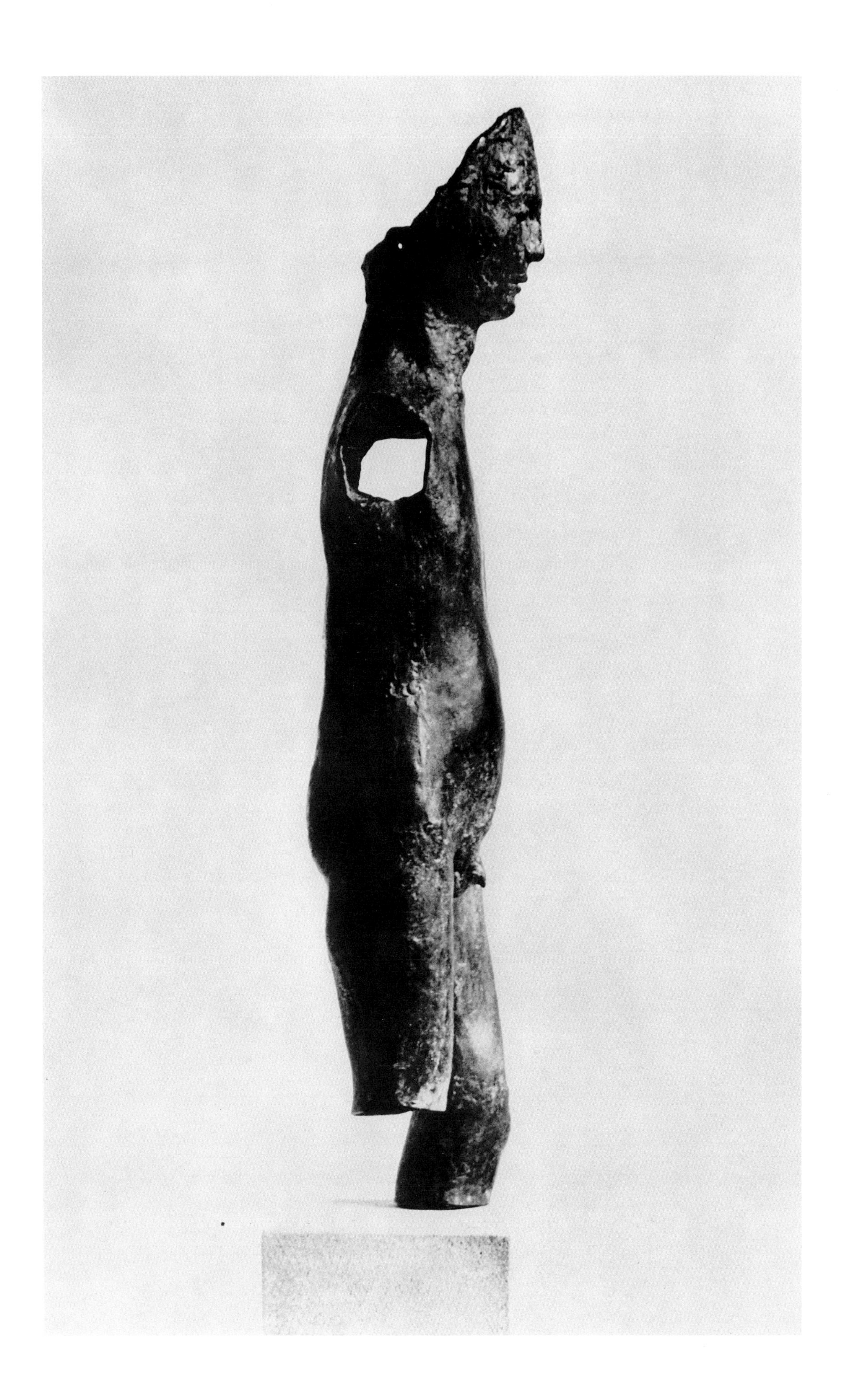

Job II

Welded Iron Rod
Height 10 Inches

1959

Collection Dr. and Mrs. Maurice Shulman, Boston, Massachusetts

Classical Head

Welded Iron Rod
Height 6 Inches

1959

Collection Mrs. Herbert C. Morris, Philadelphia, Pennsylvania

Pieta

Welded Iron Rod and Sheet
Height 5 Feet • Length 6 Feet

1959

Collection Cheekwood Art Center, Nashville, Tennessee

Pieta

Right View

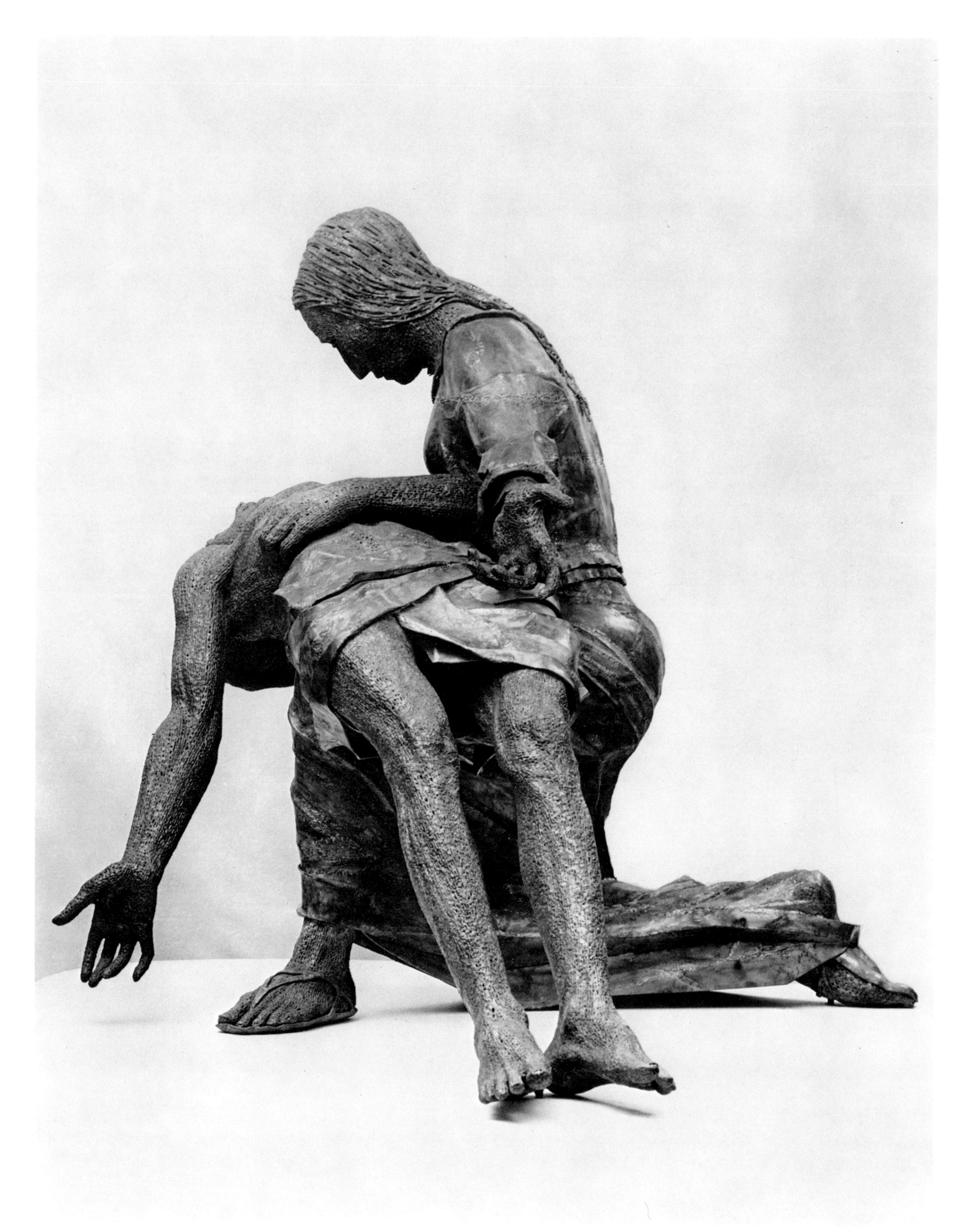

Pieta

Left View

Pieta

Rear View

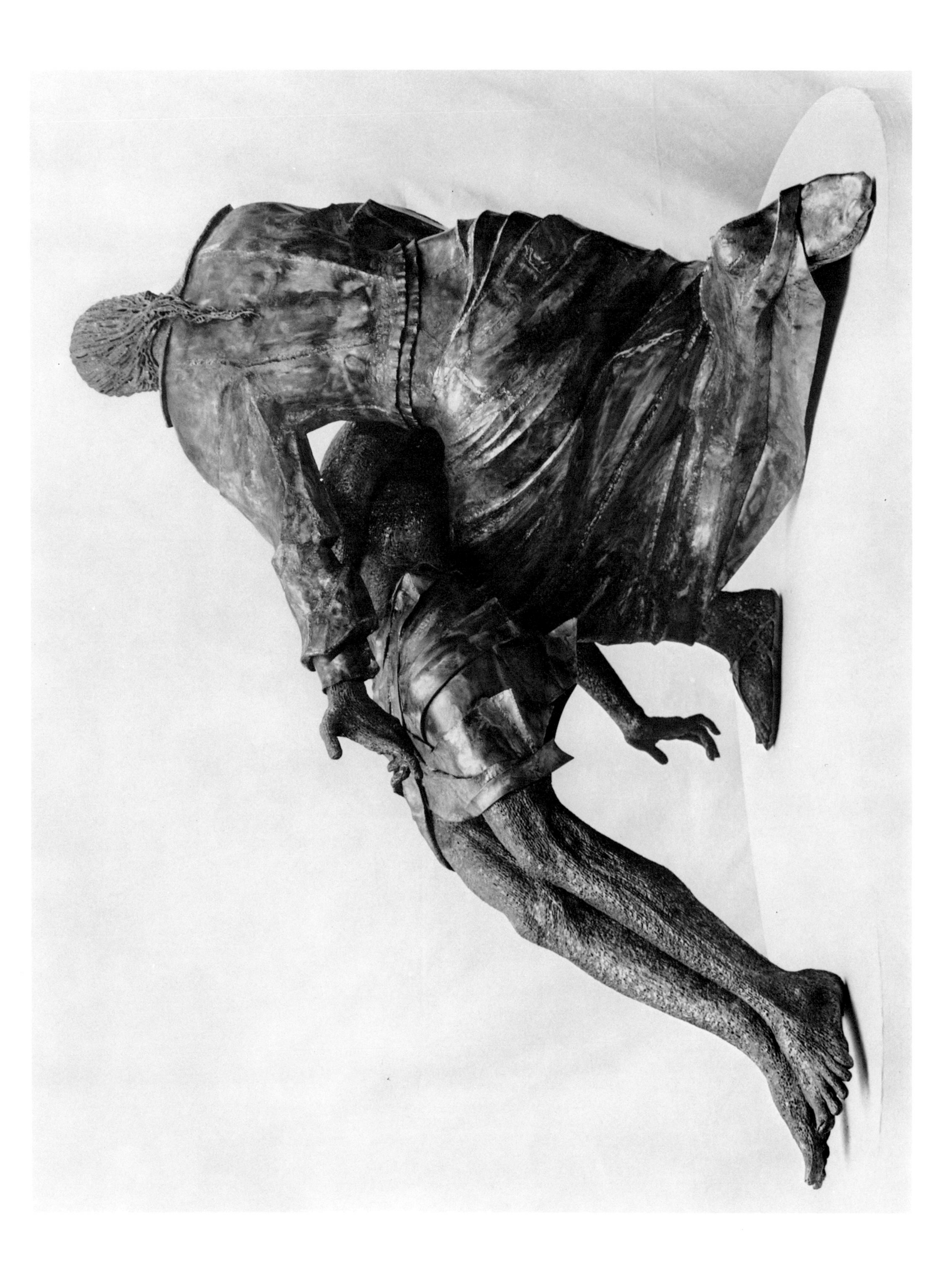

Sibelius

Hammered Steel
Height 10 Inches

1960

JUDY GOLDBERG N.Y.C.

Collection ~~Mrs. Jerry Goldberg, Brookline, Massachusetts~~

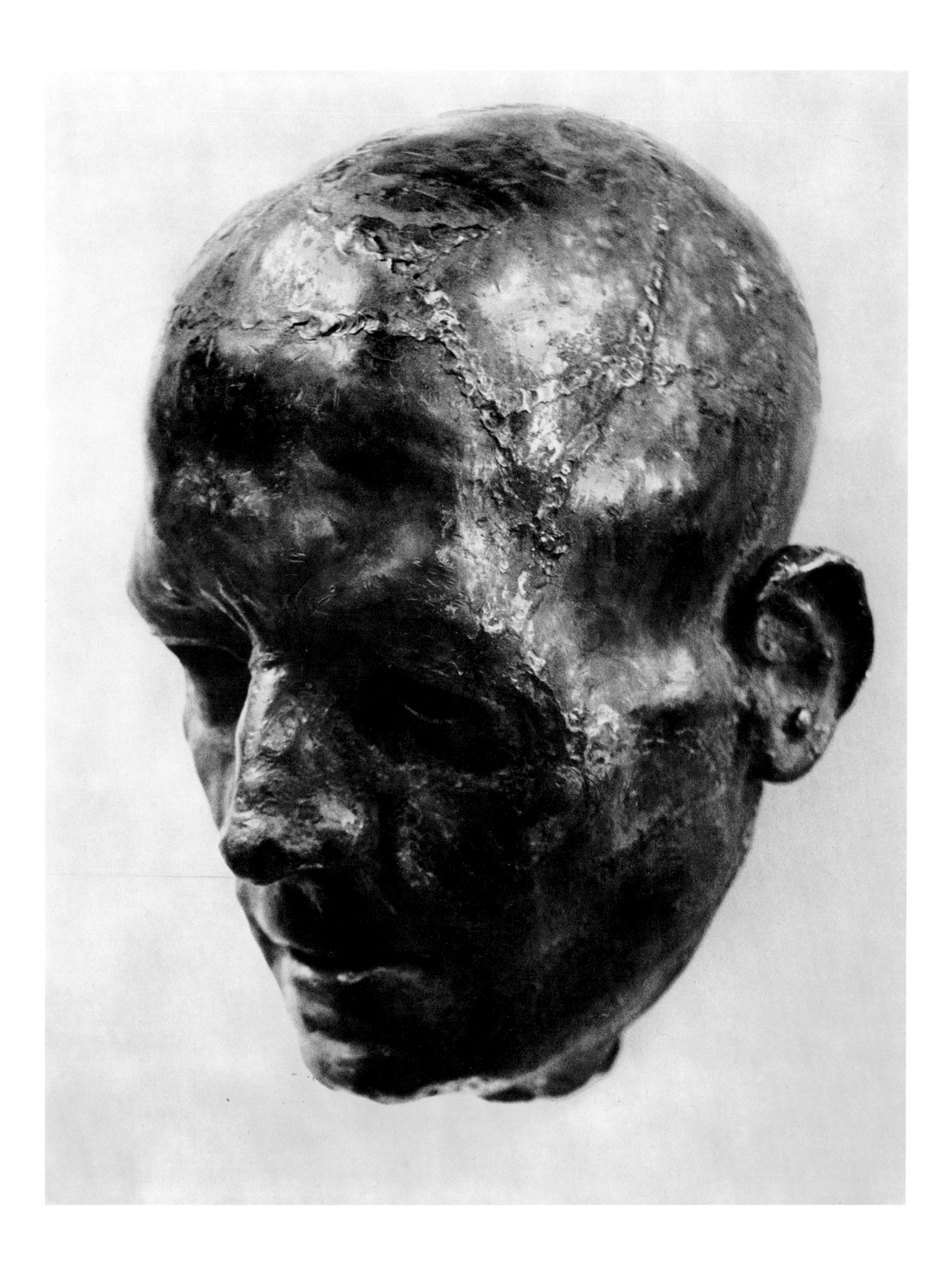

Nikki

Hammered Steel
Height 9 Inches

1960

Collection The Sculptor, Boston, Massachusetts

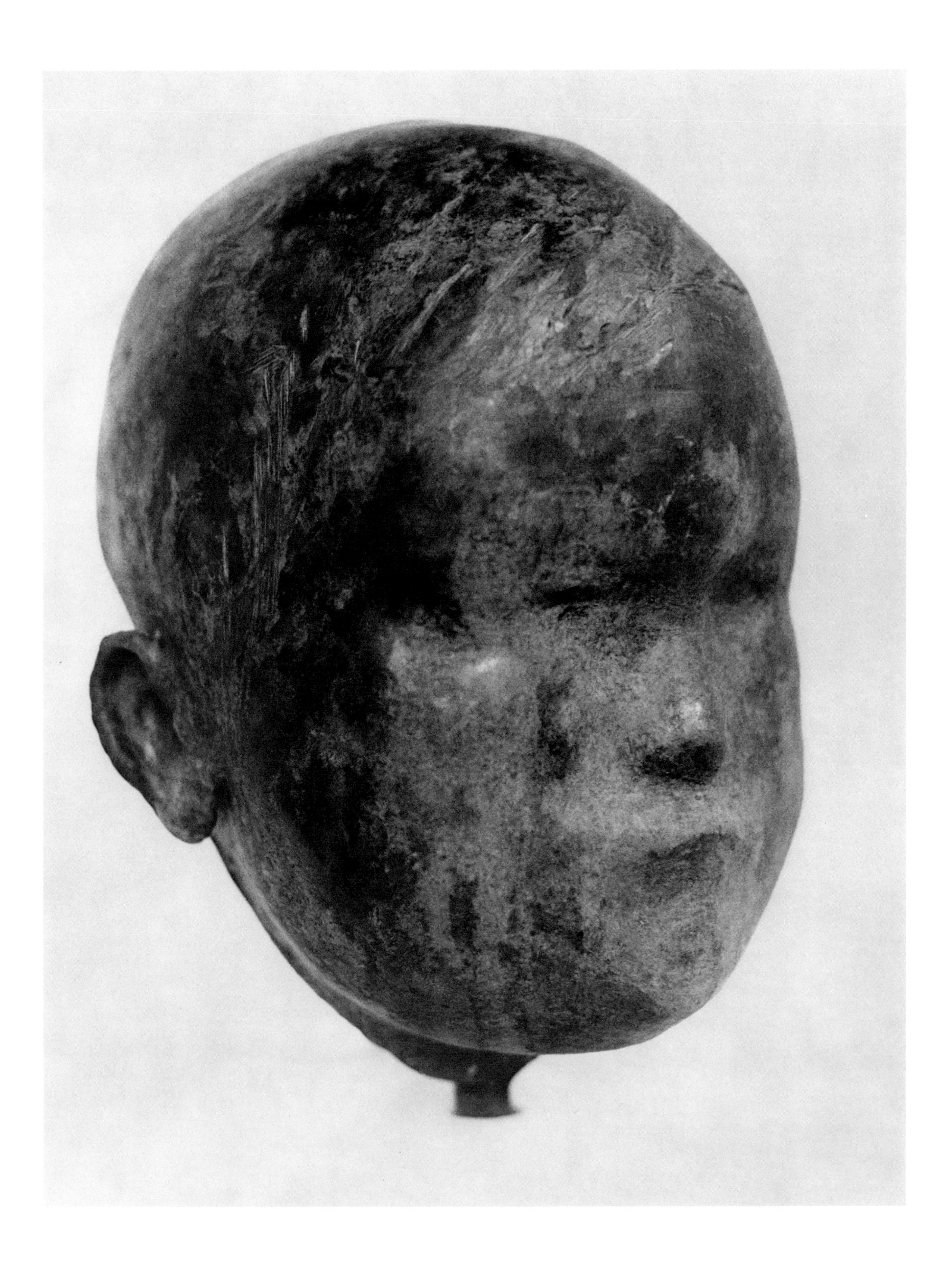

Seated Nude

Hammered Steel

Height 4 Feet • Length 3 Feet

1960

Collection William Rockhill Nelson Gallery, Kansas City, Missouri

Young Trunk

Hammered Steel
Height 23 Inches

1961

Collection ~~Mrs. Herbert C. Morris~~ LITVAC, Philadelphia, Pennsylvania

David

Hammered Steel
Height 38 Inches

1961

Collection ~~Mr. and Mrs. Walter Sharp~~ CHEEKWOOD, Nashville, Tennessee

David

Detail

Antique Head

Hammered Steel
Height 8 Inches

1961

Collection Mr. Lee Nordness, New York, New York

Borstal Boy

Hammered Steel
Height 14 Inches

1961

Collection Mr. and Mrs. William Ross, Brookline, Massachusetts

Winter's Child

Hammered Steel
Height 10 Inches

1962

Collection Mrs. Pauline Mead, Sarasota, Florida

Little Annie

Hammered Steel
Height 14 Inches

1962

Collection Mr. and Mrs. William Ross, Brookline, Massachusetts

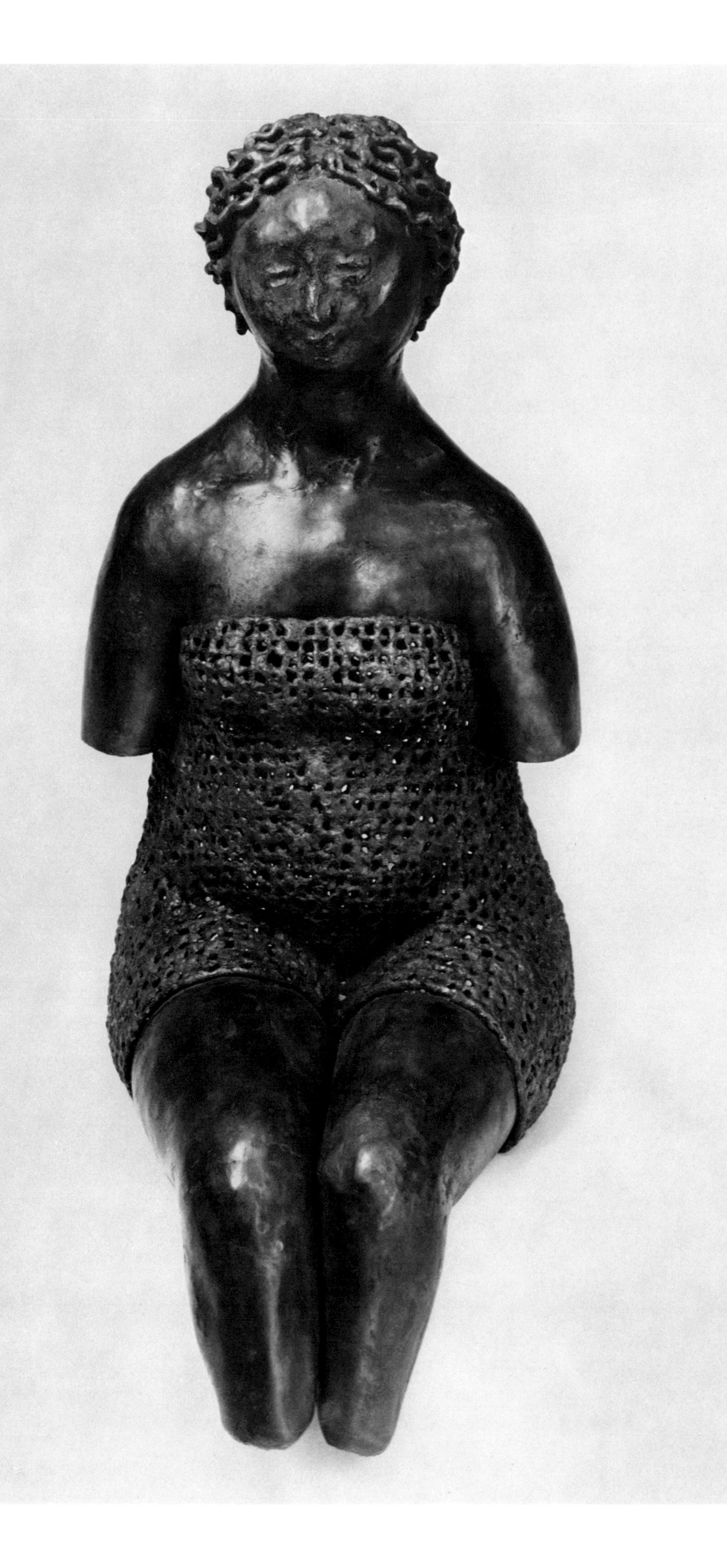

Sweet Prince

Hammered Steel

Height 10 Inches • Width 14 Inches

1962

Collection Mr. and Mrs. William Ross, Brookline, Massachusetts

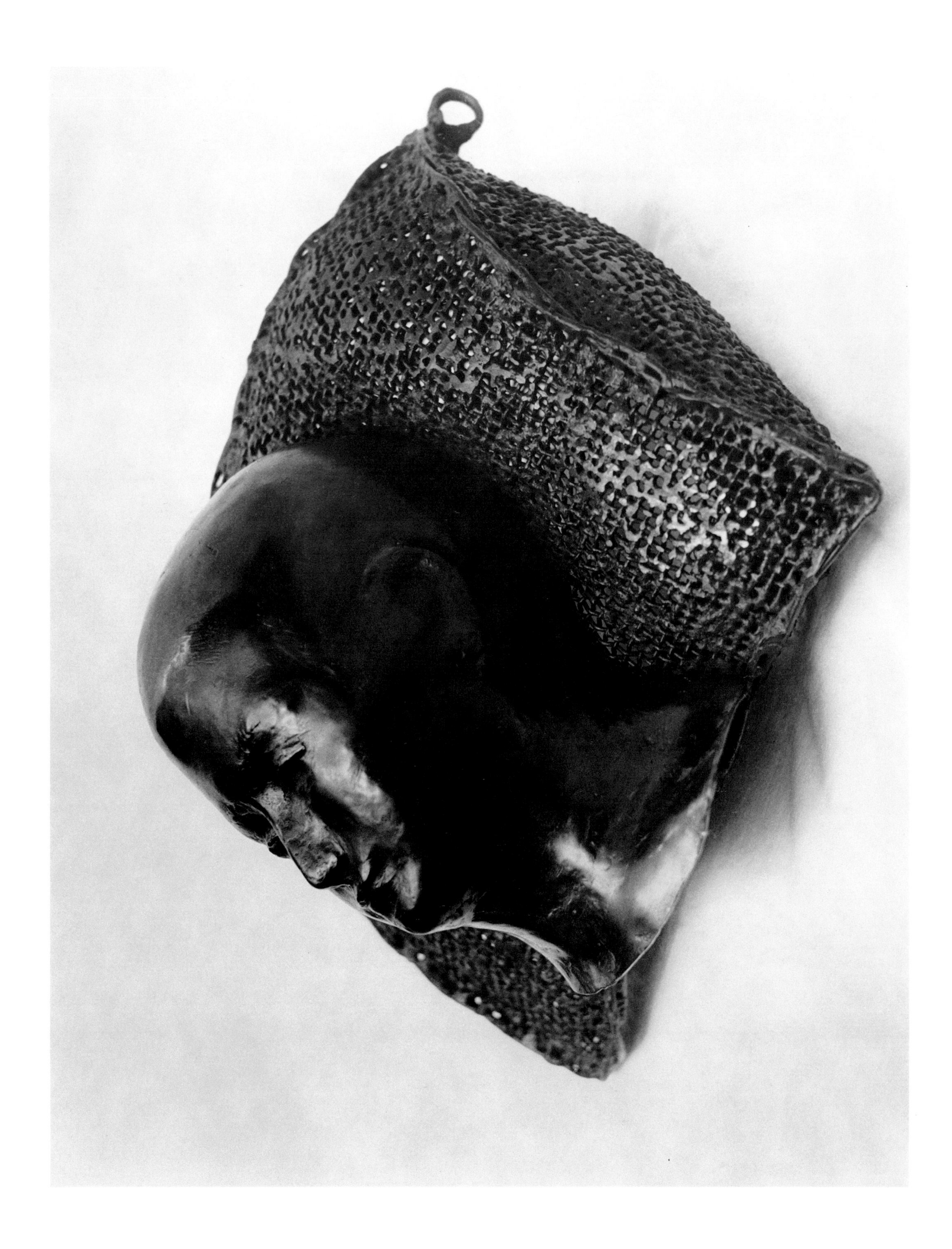

Javelier

Hammered Steel
Height 27 Inches

1962

Collection Mr. and Mrs. Walter Sharp, Nashville, Tennessee

Image of Night

Hammered Steel
Height 16 Inches

1962

Collection Mr. Hubert de Givenchy, New York, New York

Victim

Hammered Steel
Length 4 Feet 6 Inches

1963

Collection The Brockton Art Center, Fuller Memorial, Brockton, Massachusetts

Bouquet of Lillies

Welded Steel
Height 36 Inches

1963

Collection Mr. and Mrs. ~~Marshall Caras~~, Brookline, Massachusetts

Bouquet

Welded Steel
Height 30 Inches

1963

Collection Mr. and Mrs. George Sibley, Brookline, Massachusetts

Standing Plant

Welded Steel
Height 24 Inches

1963

Collection Mrs. Pauline Mead, Sarasota, Florida

Ring a' Leavo

Cast Bronze

Height 4 Feet • Width 8 Feet

1964

SHIRLEY ROSEN PALM SPRINGS CAL

Collection ~~Mr. and Mrs. Roger Sonnabend~~, ~~Brookline~~, ~~Massachusetts~~

Nureyev

Cast Bronze
Height 15 Inches

1964

Collection Mr. and Mrs. Norman B. Pierce, East Bridgewater, Massachusetts

Figure

Welded Steel
Height 6 Feet

1965

ELMIRA COLLEGE
Collection ~~Mr. and Mrs. Lee Kolker, Scarsdale~~, New York

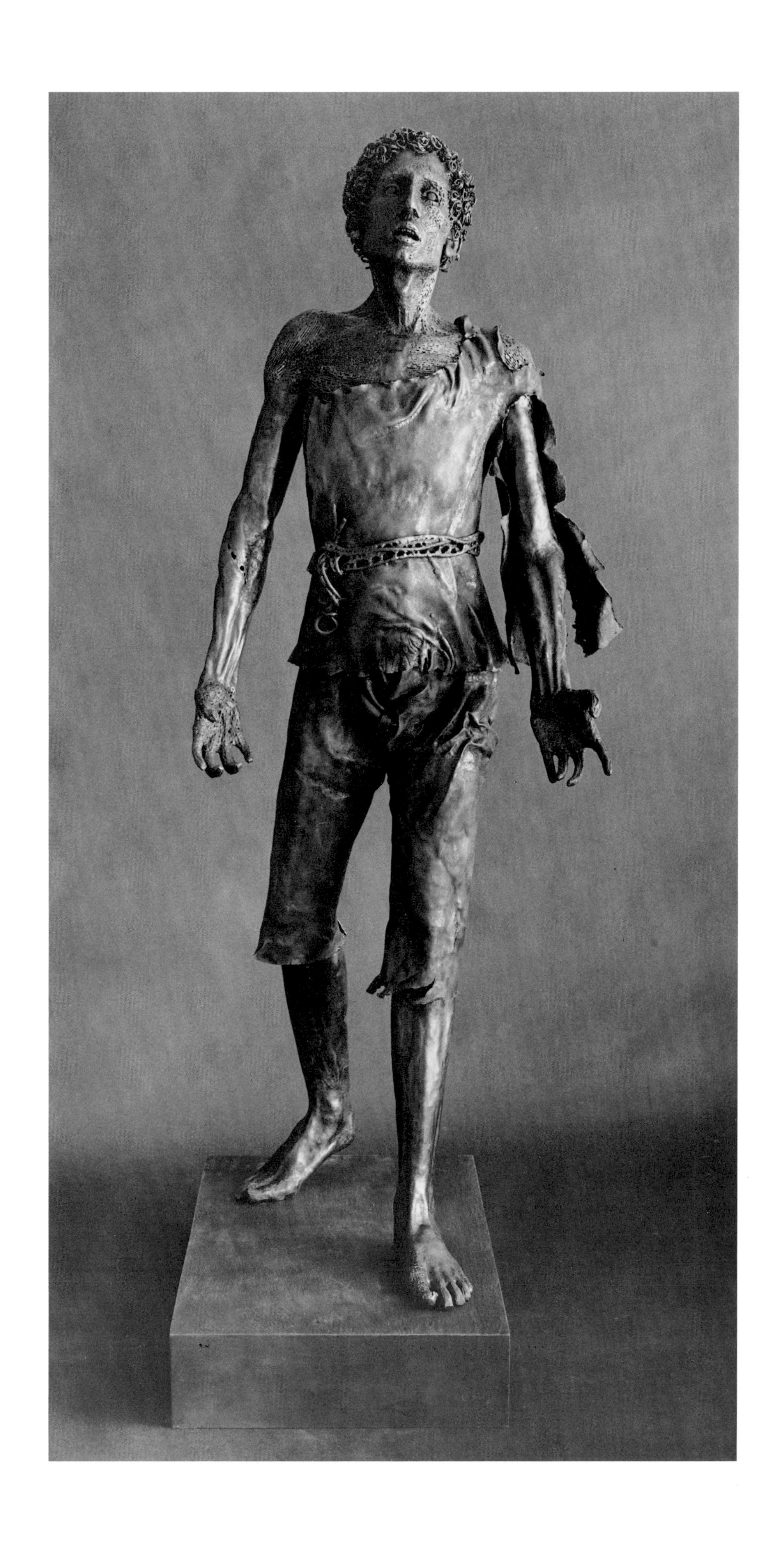

Figure

Right View

Figure

Detail

Reclining Nude

Hammered Steel

Height 3 Feet • Width 3 Feet • Length 6 Feet

1967

Collection The Sculptor, Boston, Massachusetts

Reclining Nude

End View

Reclining Nude

Top Right View

BRONZE PLAQUES

Profile of Job

Bronze

7 x 9 Inches

1969

Collection Mr. and ~~Mrs. Stuart Denenberg, Cambridge, Massachusetts~~

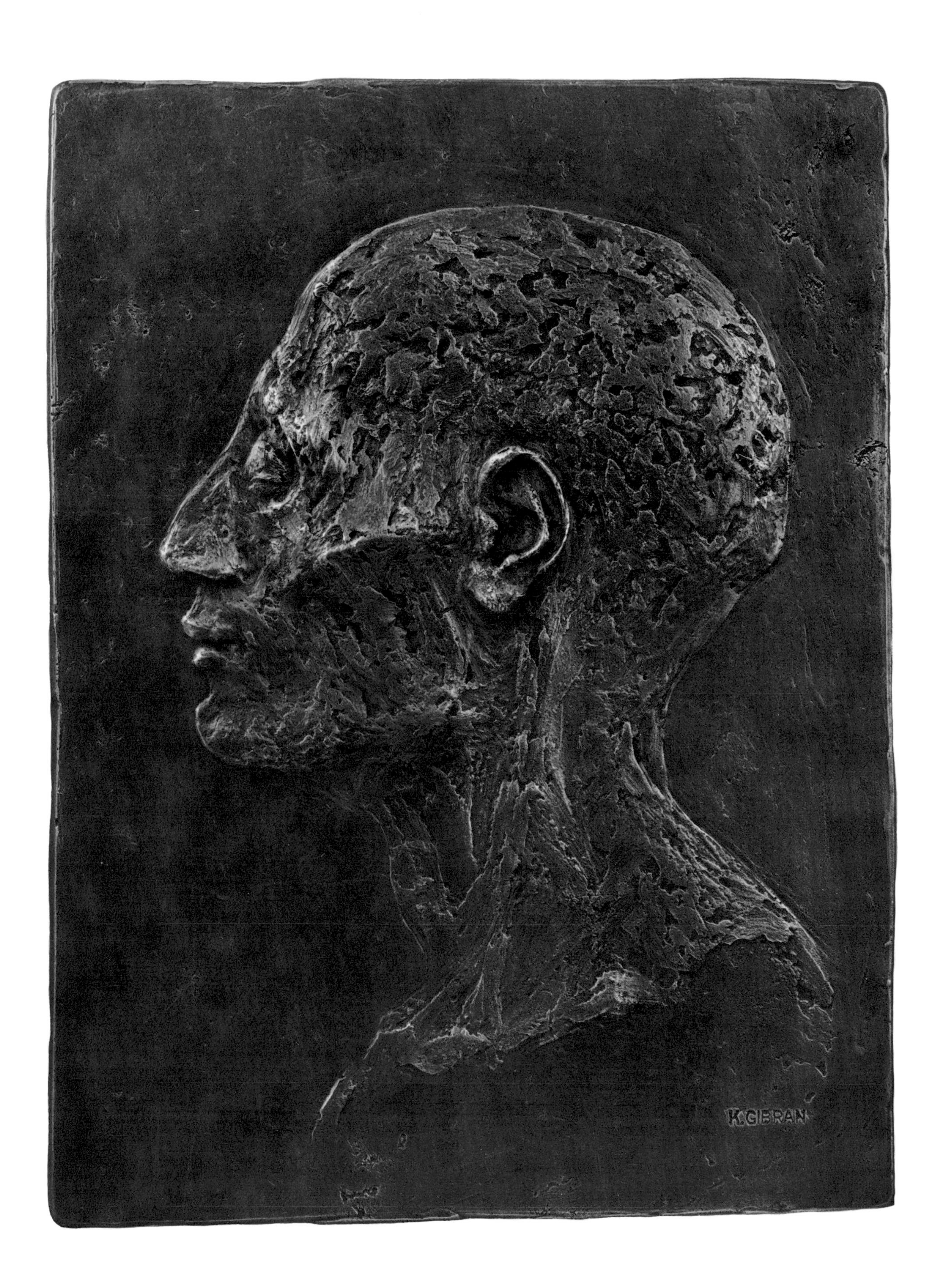
K.GIBRAN

Hairy Head

Bronze

6½ x 9 Inches

1969

Collection ~~Mr. James Mead, Boston, Massachusetts~~

K.GIBRAN

Girl with Ribbons

Bronze
8 x 12½ Inches

1969

Collection Mr. and Mrs. John Felopolous, Waban, Massachusetts

K GIBRAN

Oval Nude

Bronze
10½ x 12 Inches

1969

Collection Mr. and Mrs. Donald Rockwell, Boston, Massachusetts

Hanging Man

Bronze

7½ x 13½ Inches

1969

Collection ~~Mr. Arthur Ducharme, Boston, Massachusetts~~

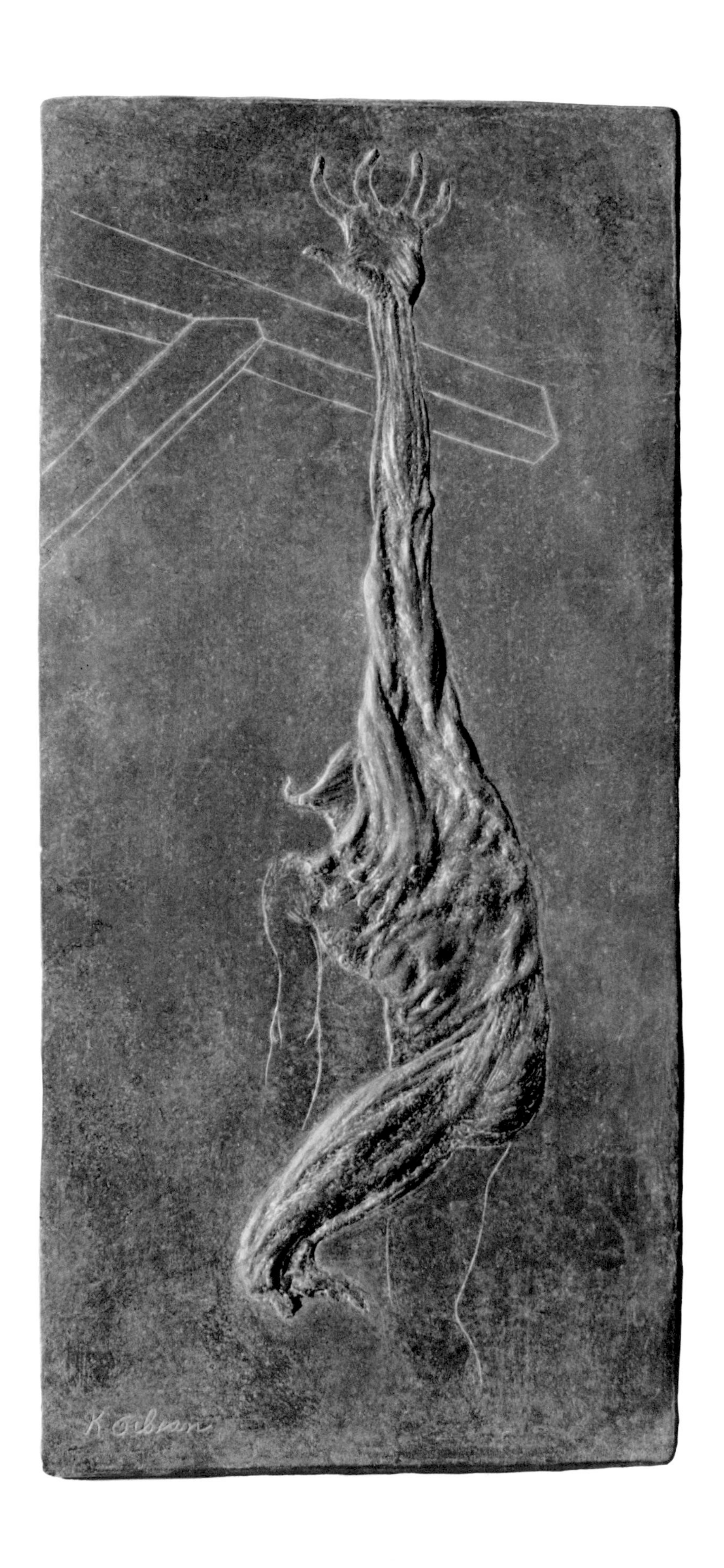
K Gibran

Old Man and Memory

Bronze

9 x 11½ Inches

1969

Collection Mr. and Mrs. Elias Berg, Bromma, Sweden

K. GIBRAN

Draped Oval

Bronze

9 x 12 Inches

1969

Collection ~~Mr. and Mrs. Ralph Trower, Brockton, Massachusetts~~

SCULPTURE IN PROCESS

Gibran with unfinished *Victim* (Page 83)

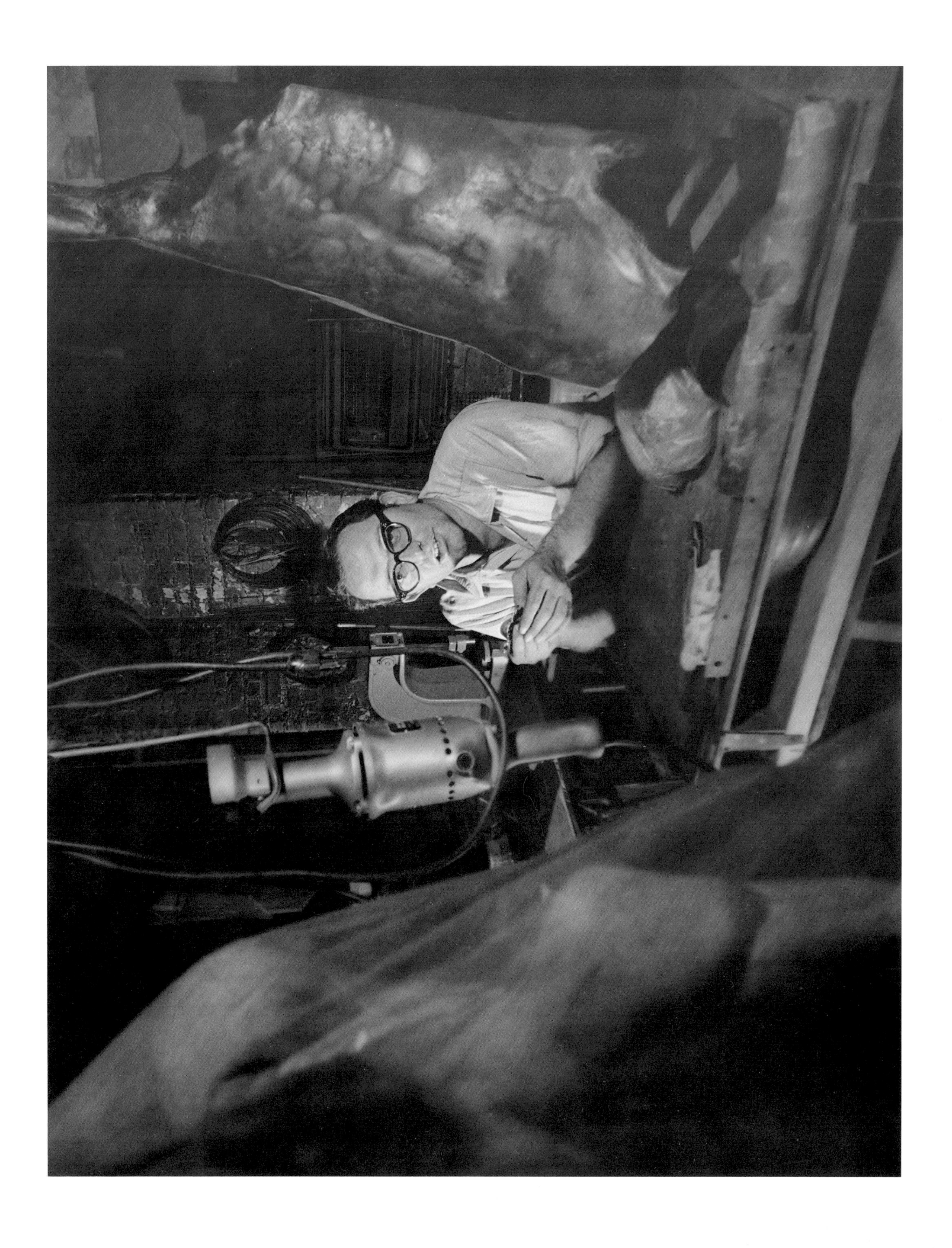

John the Baptist

Pages 15 through 21
Early stages in production

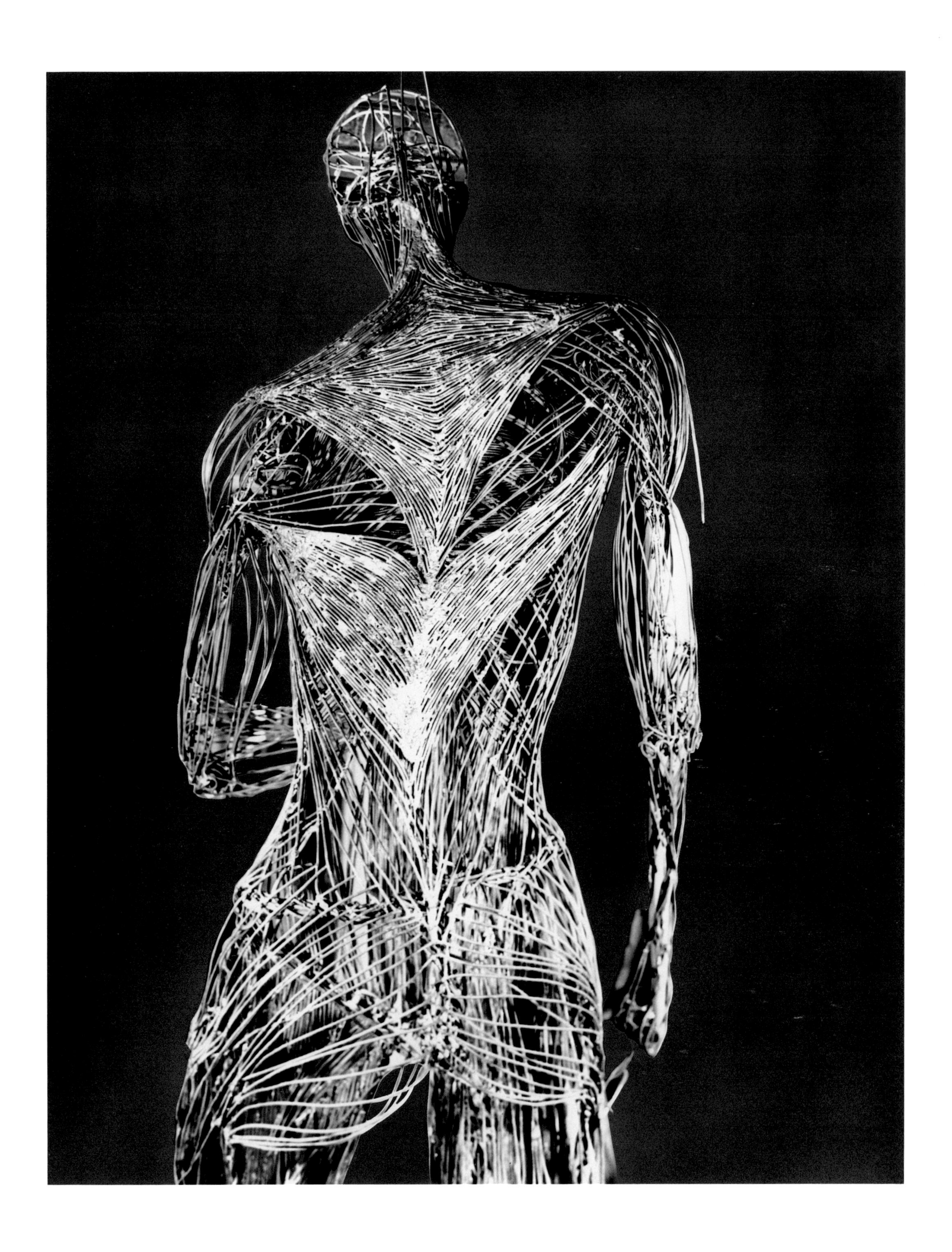

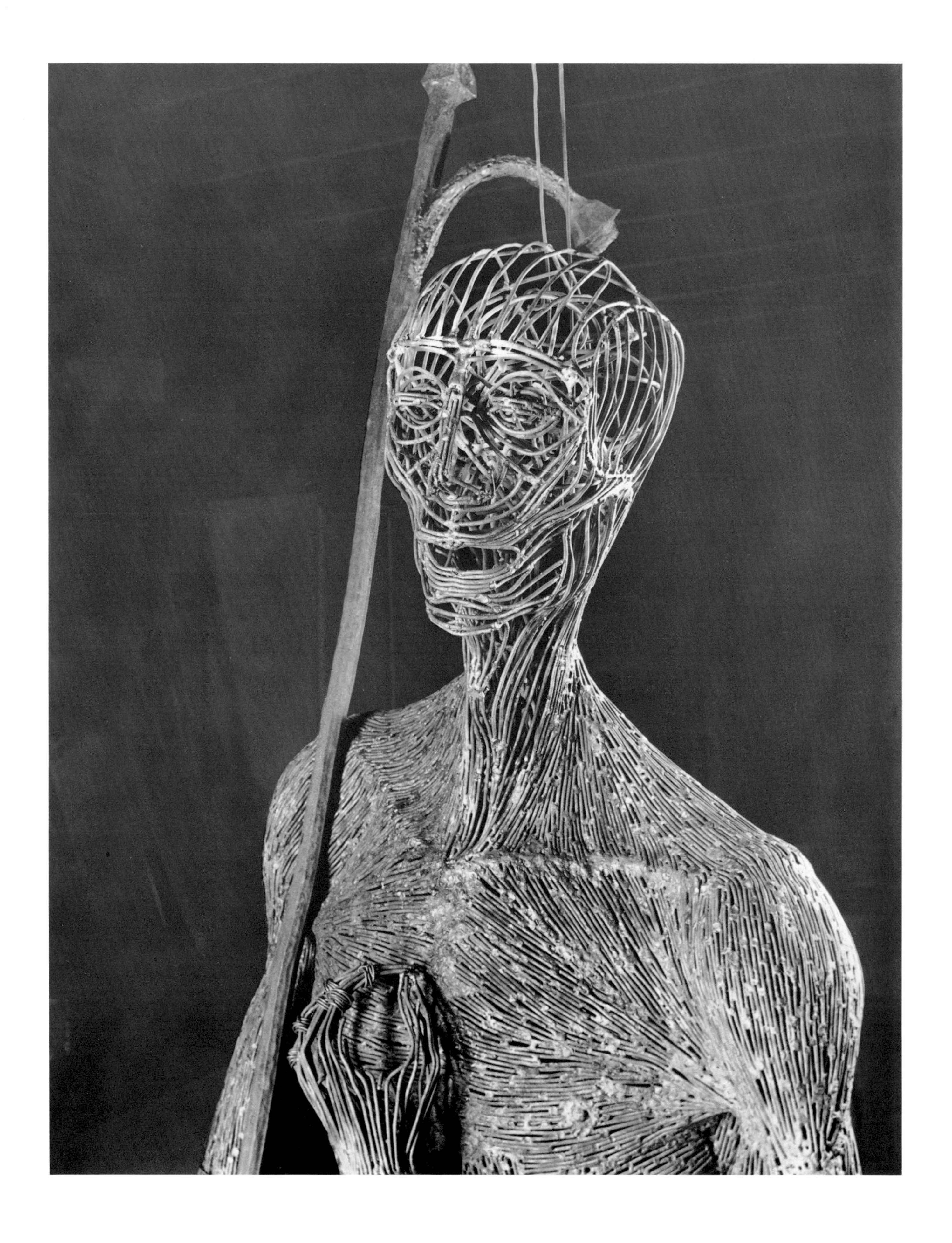

Pieta

Pages 48 through 55
Construction Details

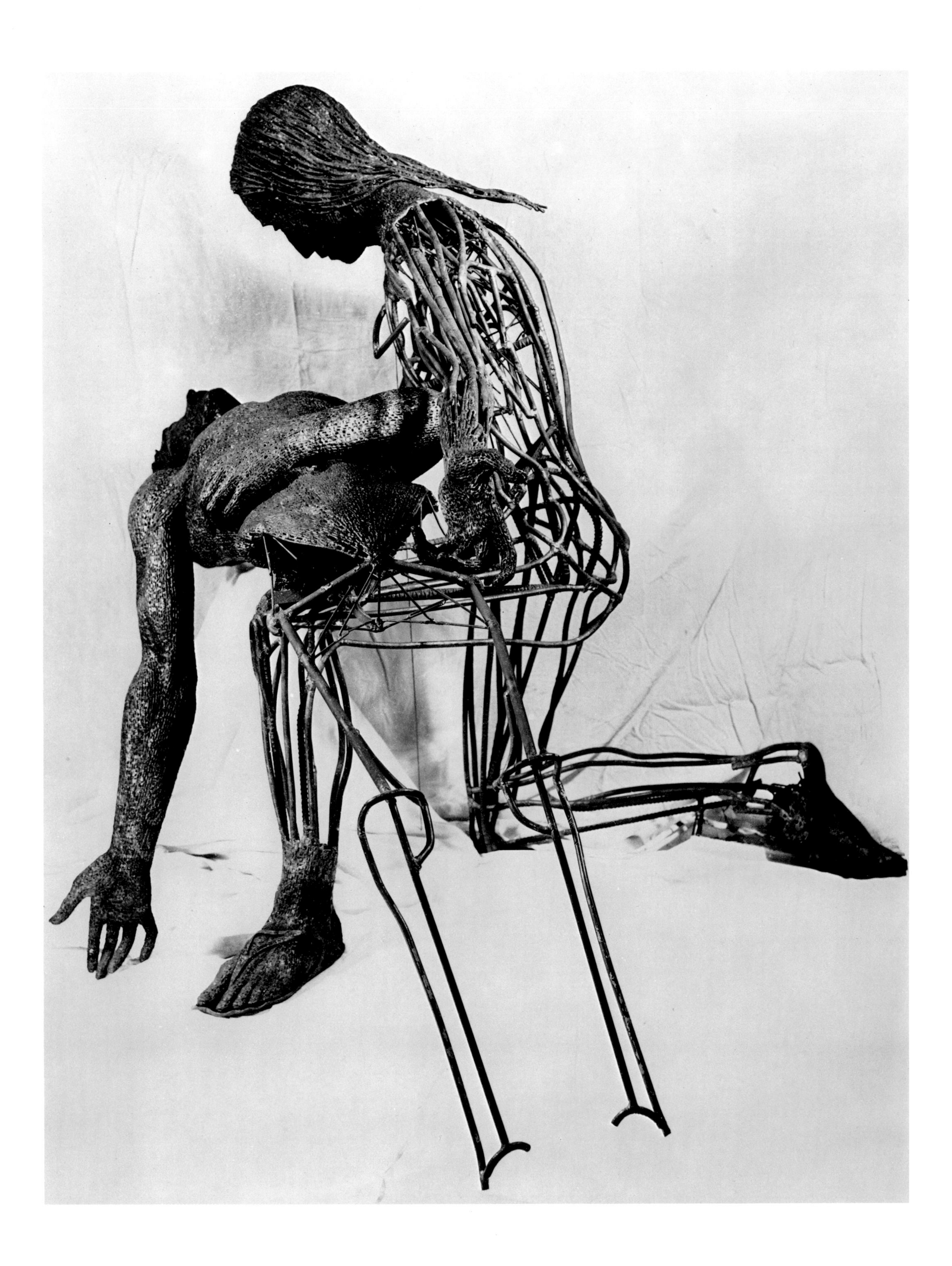

Credits

Designed by Kahlil Gibran and Morton Bartlett.
The paper is Warren's Lustro Offset Enamel Dull.
Typeset by General Composition Co. of Boston. All matter was set in Bodoni Bold, 14 pt. or smaller; the larger sizes are enlarged photographically.
Printed by The Meriden Gravure Co., Meriden, Connecticut.
Bound by Robert Burlen & Son, Inc., Boston.
Photographs:
Alan Barnett, 15, 17
Morton Bartlett, 49, 51, 53, 55, 57, 59, 61, 63, 65, 67, 69, 71, 73, 75, 77, 79, 83, 85, 87, 89, 109, 111, 113, 115, 117, 119, 121, 125, 131
Jean Gibran, 19, 21, 23, 25, 27, 29, 31, 33, 35, 37, 127, 128, 129
Kahlil Gibran, 39, 41, 43, 45, 47, 81, 93
Steve Grohe, 95, 97, 99, 101, 103, 105